T0287280

Woven Textiles of Varanasi

Woven Textiles of Varanasi

JAYA JAITLY

NIYOGI BOOKS

Published by
NIYOGI BOOKS
Block D, Building No. 77,
Okhla Industrial Area, Phase-I,
New Delhi-110 020, INDIA
Tel: 91-11-26816301, 26818960
Email: niyogibooks@gmail.com
Website: www.niyogibooksindia.com

Images & Text: Jaya Jailty
Other photo credits on page 124

Editor: Supriya Mukherjee
Design: Anupa Dasgupta

ISBN: 978-93-83098-37-8
Publication: 2014
Reprint: 2018

Printed at: Niyogi Offset Pvt. Ltd., New Delhi, India

No textile treasure can be greater than the person who weaves it.
This work is therefore dedicated to all the weavers of Varanasi,
past and present, who over time and despite many vicissitudes
have held on to their inherited skills with pride and honour.

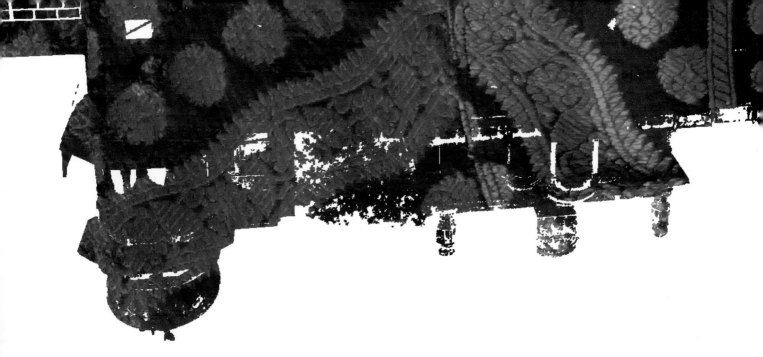

Contents

Preface

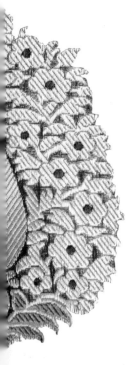

Our highest salute should go to the entire community of people involved in keeping alive the traditions of handloom weaving in Varanasi. From the lowliest weaver, who is occasionally and tragically compelled to donate his blood to earn money to feed his family, to aged women who continue to sort yarn and spin, despite wearing broken spectacles and living in penury, to the elite group of Muslim and Hindu masterweavers; add to these the zari makers, exporters, traders, shopkeepers, urban textile designers, and dedicated activists and academics, all of them are enmeshed in this collective strength that refuses to let honoured skills die. It may be a compulsion for some because there is no other option for survival in sight. Many view it simply as tradition or habit. For others it is a source of prestige, pride and earning.

Older weavers reminisce nostalgically of the days when the younger generation came to learn and worked hard to hone the skills they were taught. Today they shake their heads in disapproval and despair as they describe how young men are busier with their mobile phones than with handwork, preferring to sit at a powerloom, provided the power is on, reading a film magazine while the machine does the work. They curse computerization and cheap foreign imitations of what their old *naqshabands* and masterweavers used to

Pages 8-9: *The motif which avoids being a direct replication of a peacock is taken from a rumal, coverlet, from the 19th century displayed at the Calico Museum in Ahmedabad. It has been transposed on to a contemporary sari with equal finesse.*

Cover: *Dupatta in silk with motifs in gold zari. The motif is a contemporary adaptation of cows as seen in the famed picchwai paintings of Nathdwara.*

lovingly create. One masterweaver who owns a well-known establishment said tears had welled up in his eyes when he saw a master piece made by his forefathers hanging at the Victoria and Albert Museum in London.

I have made many trips to Varanasi over the years. The first was in 1956, the year Banaras officially became Varanasi, as a fourteen-year-old girl who had suddenly lost her father and was, in an unusual departure from tradition, taken to the holy ghats to perform the last rites and consign his ashes to the mighty River Ganga. For Hindus, this task is reserved for a son or nephew. However, being an only child, others in my matrilineal family from Kerala took an exceptional decision to place this onerous task in the hands of a young girl. Strangely, it was an empowering one for me.

The movement of the grand river flowing past with a power and determination of its own, the smell of incense, ghee and other auspicious substances thrown into a small fire at specified moments of the recitations, sending plumes of smoke rising and mingling with the white air, and the sound of chanting by a dozen of priests invoking everlasting peace for the departed soul, never went away from my inner memories although I have kept away from rituals ever since. These scenes still take place on the banks of the Ganga every day. People come from all over the world, cameras at hand, to watch this ultimate reality show of life, death, continuum and spirituality.

Pages 10-11: *A weaver working at his loom with sparse natural light can still produce an exquisite silk and zari creation fit for a bride.*

All my subsequent visits to Varanasi have been for the cause of artisans and weavers whose sad conditions, immense potential, and rich collective heritage have drawn me repeatedly to the narrowest and dirtiest by-lanes of this eternal city. At first, there was comfort in being amongst a continuing process that seemed as if it would go on forever. As years went by, the situation gradually turned grim. Looms began to lie idle, many draped with cobwebs that hung like grey garlands over wooden frames. The noise of the loud whirring of powerlooms took over from the gentler clackety-clack of the handloom. The grand *gaddidars* still sat against their bolsters on mattresses covered in white sheeting, but they began bemoaning the loss of markets. Governments sporadically came in with 'schemes' to tide over their problems. But even while metres of sumptuous cloth unravel on those white mattresses, and piles upon piles of shimmering golden-hued saris are brought out to seduce women customers, there has been an air of quiet desperation about their condition matched almost equally by their enterprising efforts to refashion production and reach out to the world as they did in better times.

For generations, the purchase of a Banarasi sari for weddings has been a matter of habit. Mine was no different. For all those women for whom sari wearing is a tradition, possessing a 'Banarasi' is a necessity. Not only does the bride have to wear a *kumkum* red, fuschia pink or flaming orange and gold brocade sari, she would also have a

Pages 12-13: *A tissue sari in pink silk with zari woven in the late 19th century. Part of her grandmother's collection, the bride wore it for her wedding ceremony in the 1960s.*

sheer 'tissue' veil woven all through with *zari* threads over her shoulders, for added modesty and adornment. The bridegroom's turban would most probably be of Banarasi silk or tissue as well. Changes in style, habits and other extraneous influences may have brought the number of customers down, but when families have to buy saris in bulk to give to a number of female relatives as part of mandatory wedding custom, the Banarasi is always the most sought after, most appreciated. It is also the handiest to collect from the myriad shops in the bustling noisy city or from the air-conditioned showrooms of the more fortunate entrepreneurs. At the same time, cries of mechanized imitations and the dumping of cheap and tawdry alternatives in the marketplace became louder. Globalization has made trade freer than it ever was in the time of the Mughals or British rule. In these processes the strong displace the weak, hands give way to machines, and creative minds give way to computer-programmed designs.

The internet allowed competitors to pick up motifs that were never a part of the local culture and conveyed no roots in any particular identity or history. As far as possible, weavers have tried to adapt and move with the times. They give the single tag 'modern' to new additions in patterns like plain dots, zigzags, stripes, bows and English roses, as against the more elaborate traditional ones with Urdu names that described soft mist, the jasmine blossom or the famed *nilambari* sari which is in a particular shade of blue-black depicting the night sky, dotted with tiny *butis* in silver and gold *zari* like stars across a luminous firmament.

Fearing that the excesses of mindless globalization would bring about the extinction of precious localized traditions in textile manufacturing, local wisdom and techniques applied to the preparation and preservation of food, medicinal herbs and compounds and other cultural expressions that form a part of a country's tangible and intangible heritage, the Government of India established the Geographical Indicators Act in December 1999. It allowed claimants to such legacies to apply for legal protection against imitations of the same name by competitors who did not belong to that area. Basmati rice, Haldiram' savouries, neem toothpaste, Chanderi saris, and Banaras brocades, among others, had all come under threat. Hard work put in by many concerned organizations and individuals won protection under the Act for Banarasi Silks in 2009. The announcement was of profound importance. It was communicated by Law Wire—Communicating the Law, among other sources, on Tuesday, September 22, 2009. I reproduce an extract from this website so that the full import of these rights can be understood:

Banarasi Silk receives GI rights (India) Banarasi silk products have been registered under Geographical Indication (GI) rights with the name `Banaras Brocades and Sarees'. This is the first ever GI status that any product in Eastern UP has received. Malihabadi Dussehri mango is another product that is enjoying GI status in the state of Uttar Pradesh. The GI rights curb others from processing or marketing any product under the same name and are as good as intellectual property rights. The GI certificate for Banarasi silk products have been received by the office of Assistant Director (Handloom) and other applicants. The certificate will prove to be advantageous for exporters and consumers, along with handloom weavers, said Mr. Rajni Kant, President, Human Welfare Association (HWA) who is also one of the applicants. As GI status is the measure to restrict the misuse of Banarasi sari brand, it would benefit around 1.2 million people who are directly or indirectly associated with handloom silk industry of the region. According to the certificate issued by the registrar of GI, Banaras Brocades and Sarees come under four classes (13-26) that include silk brocades, textile goods, silk sarees, dress material and silk embroidery. This registration is for 10 years, which can be renewed further.

However, laws may accord rights but are only instruments. They do not guarantee survival unless many other sustaining inputs are available and the Act involves processes that assist easy enforcement. For the woven treasures of Varanasi it would mean access to cotton and silk yarn at reasonable and controlled prices, an efficient route to a wide variety of markets, including international ones, better facilities and workplaces for weavers, and a concerted campaign to highlight the hidden textile treasures originating from this holy city. Understanding the differences between imitations and the real thing is also important.

While wandering along the ghats and visiting bookshops geared for tourists in Varanasi, I found many books on the Ganga, the holy city and its temples, but none on its weaving traditions that date far back in history and have been carrying on unbroken since their inception, just as the city itself has been an active living organism from an age that no history book can remember. If all who come to Varanasi to seek eternal bliss, enlightenment and salvation, took time to explore the interiors of the city where weavers proudly display their creations, they would be extending a helping hand to the tradition of fine weaving and its skilled and hardworking practitioners. My writing is to give just a small, informal glimpse of Varanasi's textile past, present and future. It hopes to share with the reader the vast potential still very much alive among the few thousand remaining looms scattered in its rural and urban workplaces.

Pages 14-15: *Detail of a wide odhni or veil, woven on a 60" wide loom in the 19th century. The pattern is made up of kairi, paisley, placed as a konia at the corners of the pallu. The broad plain chaudani pallu is outlined by mothra. The body pattern is placed diagonally.*

Varanasi Through Time

In ancient Pali scripts it was spelt Baranasi. But that was not its only name. The ancient city of India that defies time was named Avimytaka, Anandakanana, Mahasmasana, Suranshana, Brahma Vardha, Sudarsana, Ramya, Kashi, and Benaras during various periods of its rich history. In 1956 it was officially named Varanasi. Call it by any name, Varanasi still holds the same magic as when you discover an exquisitely woven, old brocade sari carefully folded between a thin layer of muslin cloth to protect it, tucked away in an old trunk.

Those who provide symbols of the modern world have attempted to install traffic lights, flyovers and billboards advertising international brands of lifestyle accessories and call it modern development. However, Varanasi's inner core remains the same. The popular mindscape of Varanasi is of the ever flowing, ever changing silver-flecked river Ganga, the deep sounding temple bells, the crowded *ghats* where prayers rise up for those recently deceased or of those hoping for *moksha*. The aura of eternity hovers like a haze of incense over the city—albeit near the piles of refuse everywhere. You soon come

Page 18: Visitors to Varanasi can take boat rides at dawn and watch the sunrise over calm, silvery waters.

to narrow winding lanes that create a maze at one's feet and only ribbon-strips of light when you look up to the sky. They remind you that the ancient quality of Varanasi never goes away. Thousands of people from all over the world flock to this crowded, noisy, yet indestructible city, drawn by that extra quality of antiquity and spirituality that is lacking in most parts of the world.

What could be more magical than to be in the oldest inhabited city in the world? It goes about its business, busy with today, seemingly oblivious of its ancient status, but unconsciously carrying out practices steeped in tradition and history. This ancient city sits on the bank of *Ganga Maiyya*, Mother

Ganga, the River Ganga or Ganges, as it came to be known in the western world. The very foundation of Hinduism encompasses a reverence for water, fire, the sun, the soil and nature in all its living forms. The aspect of sacredness is necessary to keep flowing water pure and unpolluted for the lives and health of civilizations living beside it and needing it for their very sustenance. Varanasi has attained the position of being the holiest of all cities in India. To die in Varanasi is to attain immediate salvation.

Above: *The ghats of Varanasi at evening time, when prayers are recited and lamps are lit.*

Above: *Lamps, flowers, ghee and incense form the basic ingredients for any ceremony in Varanasi.*

Those on the verge of death are given a few drops of Ganga water on their tongue to liberate them from the suffering of earthly bonds and merge with the divine. The lord of the city is Shiva, enshrined in the famed Kashi Vishwanath Temple. On the night of Shivratri, long queues of people carrying Ganga *jal* wait to offer it to the temple. The town is further dotted with temples dedicated to many gods, goddesses and spiritual beings who serve as protectors against evil, illness, or disaster. Sounds of temple bells, recitations and prayers are interwoven with the sounds of the muezzin calling at dawn or dusk joining the tinkle of cow bells as these gentle creatures nudge aside pedestrians to claim their right of way on the narrow winding streets. A claim asserted by the fact that they are garlanded with marigolds and a vermillion streak is drawn on their foreheads to sanctify their special status. Varanasi, in any form and for anybody is always sacred, special and a continuum of experiences that present reality within a new ambience. Sitting at dawn observing as the sun rises over the Ganga, the noise of the city disappears and a golden calm fills the surrounding atmosphere. A boatman steers his boat quietly along the edge of the calm waters. A peacock calls out and dances, turning around slowly as its feathers spread out wider and wider. There is something immediate and chaotic about Varanasi and equally there is an inner quietness, a deep sense of being that is hard to shake away.

Varanasi has attained the position of being the holiest of all cities in India. To die in Varanasi is to attain immediate salvation.

Mark Twain, the pen name of Samuel J Clemens, the American author who was always fascinated with India, wrote about Varanasi in 1897, 'Banaras is older than tradition, older even than legend, and looks twice as old as all of them put together'. The antiquity of Varanasi is said to date back to the Rig-Veda, about 1500 to 2000 BC. It was already called the ancient city when Lord Buddha began his preaching there in 500 BC.

Varanasi is mentioned in a hymn by Sri Veda Vyasa , who was born 5,500 years ago. Vyasa is among the most important figures in Hinduism, revered for having simplified the reading of the Vedas by splitting them into four parts, and for having authored the Mahabharata, of which the Gita is the most sacred. Interestingly Vyasa is both the author and a character in the Mahabharata. Vyasa is also considered to be a part incarnation of Lord Vishnu. Guru Purnima, an important Hindu festival, is dedicated to him. Vyasa's hymn referring to Varanasi reads thus:

Page 22, above: *A quiet section on the ghats beside the River Ganga encourages thoughtfulness and meditation.*

Page 22, below: *There are many ghats along the banks of the River Ganga. This is the Jain Ghat.*

Ganga-taranga-ramaneeya-jataakalaapam,

Gauri-niranta-vibhushita-vaamabhaagam,

Narayanapriyam-Ananga-madaapaharam,

Varanasi-purapatimbhaja Vishwanatham.

Sage Vyasa's devotional verses referring to the Ganga and Varanasi.

Pages 26-27: *Prayers on the banks of the River Ganga reach a pitch on festival days or during special ceremonies commissioned by individuals. Crowds are drawn to the chanting of prayers, the drama of flickering oil lamps and an atmosphere of spirituality in the hope of gaining benefit from it.*

Pages 24-25: *The elegant design of two peacocks on either side of a central flower motif is derived from a pattern on a torque (neck collar) in minakari jewellery. The woven pattern consists of gold and silver zari and blue silk thread. Just as stones are inlaid on gold, the thread is inlaid on the base fabric to create the motif in a twill weave.*

Above: *The narrow streets of Varanasi leading to the Kashi Vishwanath Temple are flanked by shops that sell materials required for religious ceremonies. There are also plenty of cheap ornaments, wooden toys crafted in Varanasi, and an occasional sari shop.*

Page 29: *Pre-packed offerings of sweets and savouries are sold in small plates made of leaves by families whose livelihoods depend on the religious practices in this ancient city.*

While Varanasi is firmly established as one of the oldest cities, what is often missed is that it is also home to one of the oldest textile weaving traditions in the world.

Here again, the Vedas refer to *hiranya*, gold cloth, the weaver as *tantuvay* or *tantividyas* and to the female weaver as *siri*. The gods were said to have been decked in *hiranya* as they set forth in their chariots. These probably referred to the brocades or *kinkhabs* and the *zari* of today.

The clothes that men and women wore called *neevi* referred to the undergarments, and the *baharivas* referred to the cloth which was worn to cover the body rather like what is known today as the *chadar* or shawl.

In the Rig Vedas the shawl was also called the *adivas*. Old texts repeatedly refer to the cotton textiles of Varanasi, as *angutranika*, *kasikavastra*, *kasikansu*, *kasikurtam* and *kashya*, indicating their importance in the economic and cultural life of the people, and describing them as soft, fine and soothing to the touch. Silk cloths were referred to as *kasek* or *varankasek*, and were worn with great pride by the noble gentry.

The Ramayana and Mahabharata refer to the fabric woven in Varanasi as *Hiranya Vastra* or *Putambar Vastra*. The fabric of Varanasi has been worn by kings and queens around the world and lovingly possessed by brides in nearly every household of India even in present times.

The Ramayana and Mahabharata refer to the fabric woven in Varanasi as Hiranya Vastra or Putambar Vastra. The fabric of Varanasi has been worn by kings and queens around the world and lovingly possessed by brides in nearly every household of India even in present times.

Varanasi is among the holiest destinations for Hindus, but it has also drawn Buddhists and Jain pilgrims to its fold. Pali literature of the Buddhist period often refers to the textiles of Varanasi as *Kasikuttama* and *Kasiya*.

Page 31: *An orange silk tissue sari with borders and a fine checked pattern in zari has a border and pallu in what is termed a chaudani pattern, woven in the early 19th century.*

Pages 32-33: *Cream and gold textile woven around the late 18th or early 19th century in hand spun khadi of 250 counts. Finely woven, transparent, soft and flowing, similar pieces are displayed at the Bharat Kala Bhavan in Varanasi and at the Calico Museum in Ahmedabad. The speciality of this piece lies in the pattern being woven mostly in thread with some areas in zari. In other regions only threads are used for patterning. Later, zari was exclusively used for patterning, making it less sophisticated than this piece which shows a judicious balance between thread and zari and restraint in its embellishment.*

Pages 34-35: *Pieces from old collections show the slow development of the cream and gold idea. Gradually the use of zari increases, while the base cloth is less transparent.*

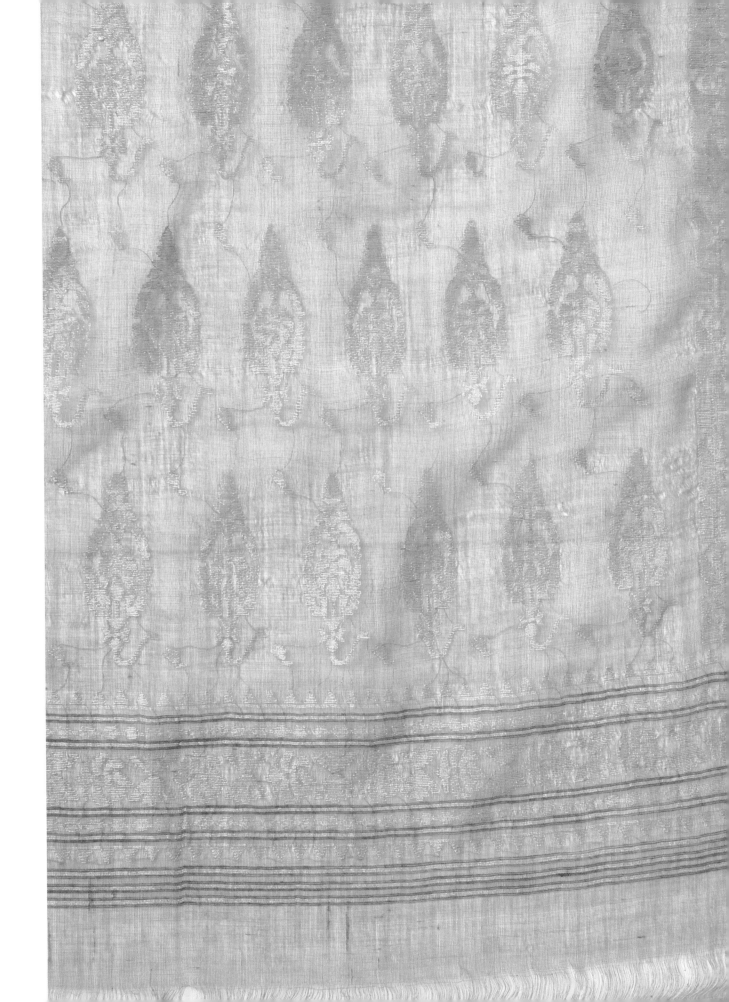

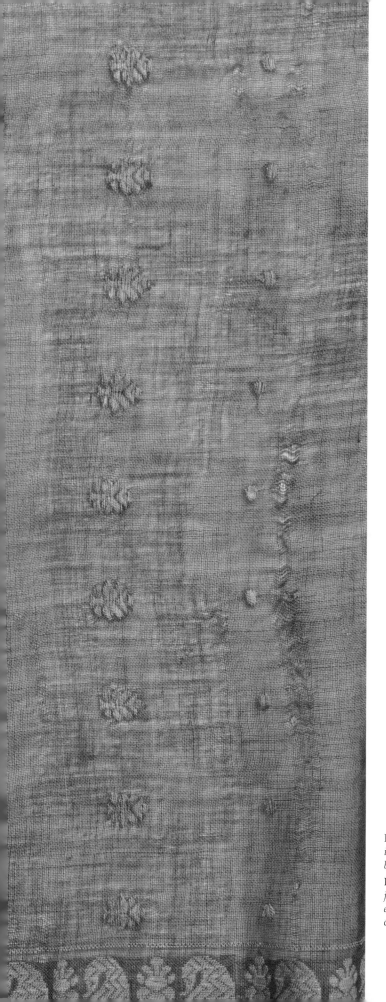

Pages 36-37: *The evolution of the cotton jamdani is complete. Woven in the early 20th century, the count is thicker, and thread patterning has been completely replaced by zari.*

Pages 38-39: *A mid 20th century sari in cotton. This finely woven jamdani with indigo dyed yarn has a pattern in kadua which means 'like embroidery' and is different from katru or cutwork. The threads are left connected on the underside.*

A Buddhist text known as the *Divyavadan* refers to *KasikaVastra, Kasikamsu*. A fine textured fabric known as *Varaaseyaka* is also mentioned.

The *Kasika Suchivastra* is said to be a kind of embroidery which could have been an embellished or raised form of weaving. Important texts make note of textiles and other arts if they are sacred or deeply ingrained in the cultural and social lives and hierarchies of the people.

Fabric is part of the story of Prince Siddharth in which it is said that he removed his royal silk robes, undoubtedly among the best that the weavers of Kasi created, and took to wearing the *Kasayanivastrani*, the simple robes of a monk.

Literature with the Maha Bodh Society that goes back 2,600 years describes the event of Gautam Buddha's cremation in which his body was wrapped in fine cloth woven in Sarnath where Buddha is said to have begun his teachings.

The Jataka Tales are a prominent part of the early Pali texts that form the collection of sacred Buddhist literature. There are around 550 fables depicting earlier incarnations of the great being who would become Siddhartha Gautama, the future Buddha.

It describes values and attributes that the Buddha attained in all his incarnations. The accepted birth and death dates of Gautama are 563-483 BC.

The Jataka tales are dated between 300 BC and 400 AD. Buddha began his teaching at Sarnath adjoining the city of Varanasi. The Jataka tales also throw light on the weaving traditions and their practitioners, the *tantuvidyas*. Their associations and guilds and the outstanding quality of their work is repeatedly mentioned giving us the historical significance of the weaving tradition of Varanasi at that time.

Shifting focus for a glimpse into the relationship between Buddhism and Varanasi today, we find that the resplendent brocade, *thiugyamo*, a cloth commonly known as *gyaser*, used by important religious Buddhist establishments across the world have been woven in Varanasi for centuries. Selected weavers continue to supply this rich textile to clients and proudly display photographs of themselves with His Holiness the Dalai Lama.

Above: *A stupa at Sarnath, in the suburbs of Varanasi.*

Page 40: *Gyaser, the heavily inlaid cloth used by Buddhists for monasteries, ceremonial dressing and other ornamentation, including the framing of tankha paintings, has been traditionally made in Varanasi.*

The fabric earlier came in 10" strips but was later developed for wider looms to fulfil the large demand that came from Tibet. Elders like Kasim of a prominent weaving house called Kasim Silks fondly recount the links between the Muslim weaving community and Tibetan monasteries that constantly required their textiles.

Prior to 1959, ancestors of the present weavers used to travel to Kalimpong (in the Darjeeling area of present West Bengal) to obtain samples from China and bring them to Varanasi to be copied. Some even took rented houses in Kalimpong to receive the woven *gyaser* from Varanasi and despatch them on the backs of ponies along a narrow track to Lhasa. The technique of weaving the *gyaser* also identifies it under the name of *kinkhab* which is the result of a technique where the base fabric is completely overlaid and has a pattern made of gold and silk threads. It is therefore very heavy and can be used only for ceremonial or religious trappings

Page 42, all images: *The relationship between Muslim weavers like Kasim and the Tibetan people, presently represented by Tenzin Gyatso, His Holiness the 14th Dalai Lama, has always been a close one. A photograph of the elder brother of the Kasim household with His Holiness is lovingly framed and hung on the wall of the Kasim Silks showroom.*

Page 43: *Tibetan symbols, borders and patterns are used by Varanasi weavers to create thousands of metres of fabric for Buddhists around the world for centuries. Today, skilled weavers are in short supply.*

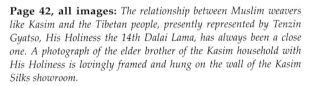

or drapes. The patterns in brocade, in contrast, are scattered, leaving areas where the weft is finer and plain and the patterns alone have a warp and weft that is double. The fabric being lighter in weight is suitable for clothing and particularly the undraped sari.

One fine *kinkhab* piece, which today hangs in the Victoria and Albert Museum in London, was given an award by the British Government in 1886. Kasim has this certificate framed and hung on his showroom wall. The weavers say that even though they are known for their sari weaving, they need workers who must be well skilled to work on this special cloth.

They complain that willing weavers are hard to find these days, but choose to continue producing the *gyaser* because it is associated with religion and, according to them 'religion can never end'. In the old days, silk yarn and metallic gold threads, *zari*, for the *gyaser* came from Japan, but now they use Indian substitutes of lower quality to supply cloth to monasteries all over the world. Their customers come regularly from as near as Sarnath and as far as Tibet.

Interestingly, their age-old links with Tibet brought them out on the streets in solidarity when Tibetans protested the holding of the Olympic Games in China in 2008. For these weavers of Varanasi, the end of Tibetan culture and religion, if the authorities in China had their way, would be the end of their livelihoods and historical linkages. Kasim also proudly tells visitors that they made the

biggest *tankha* ever, for the Phyang Gompa in Ladakh and that it went in a special aircraft from Varanasi.

The heavier *gyasers* are used for ceremonial costumes of dancers. Long lengths of fabric used drapes in monasteries. Many Buddhist religious and cultural establishments paint *tankhas* which are embellished by framing them with *gyaser* fabric. These hand painted *tankhas* are either framed or, more popularly used as scrolls. Not only are these made more valuable when the *gyaser* is of shimmering hand woven fabric but adds to its worth as an important art piece.

Use of cotton was pre-dominant in early times as the surrounding regions were cotton growing, but by the 5th and 6th century, waste silk fibres from wild silk worms along with hemp were used for weaving fabric in Varanasi. Fine, smooth silk yarn was produced apart from the best of cotton but the basic foundation of extremely skilled weaving in cotton had been laid well before that. The tradition of handloom weaving in Varanasi which had been deep and well-established from very early times continued to be patronized and developed by succeeding kingdoms of the Nandas, the Mauryas, the Guptas and the Sungas, which are described in the writings of

Patanjali in the 2nd century BC and referred to as the *Kasika* textile.

When studies were carried out to date the weaving traditions of Varanasi to prove its antiquity at this location, it was found that patterns carved on the Sarnath stupa were transferred to textile designs in the Gupta period. According to this study, 'A number of such motifs appearing on the Dhamekh-Stupa at Sarnath in Varanasi presuppose the transference of the textile designs on stone or a copy of some textiles which originally wrapped such stupas'. These textiles were called Devadushyas.

The Gupta period also describes a calendaring process that is used till today. Descendants of those artisans who used this process to stiffen and make smooth the woven cotton cloth live in Kundigar Zola in Varanasi and can be observed working in the same manner as was done in the 8th and 9th centuries.

Above: *The condition of the weaver does not match the richness of the fabric he weaves.*

Page 44: *A tankha painting framed with Varanasi-made gyaser and hung as a scroll.*

Above: *A painting of the Raja of Kollengode, by renowed Indian artist Amrita Sher-Gil in the early 20th century, shows him wearing an achkan tailored in the style introduced by the Mughals using a brocade fabric from Varanasi.*

Page 47: *A jacket fashioned out of hand woven textile locally called tashi brocade. Being a Tibetan word it is possibly linked to a design used for weaving gyaser cloth.*

Mughal History

Mughal rule in India, from 1526 to 1717, was when Indian textiles suitable for courts and the display of ceremonial splendour achieved their greatest heights. This was a period of enrichment for many practitioners of India's arts and crafts since Emperor Akbar and others paid special attention to the development of arts, crafts and textiles in India in many creative arts. Artisans shared skills they had learned in Persia. They brought Persian carpet weavers, embroiders, fine artists and craftsmen of almost every category, who fused their knowledge and styles with those already existing in India. This brought about a tradition of Muslims making artefacts and fabrics for Hindus and vice versa, leading to an integration and harmony both in design and society. The textiles of Varanasi were no exception. Many fabrics were created not only for the Mughals in India but for Safavid Iran in the 17th and 18th centuries.

Though Islam has no caste, when Hindus from different castes converted to Islam they divided themselves into upper and lower castes, with the Ansaris, also known as Julahas taking over the bulk of handloom weaving. Even today, they would probably represent ninety percent of the weaving community. Thus they were both a community as well as a professional grouping.

Naqshabands, pattern makers, who would today be called designers, would draw intricate designs prepared on a small loom to be followed by the weaver on the larger draw loom. The original designs were drawn on sheets of mica with a steel pen. Later they were made on paper and finally placed

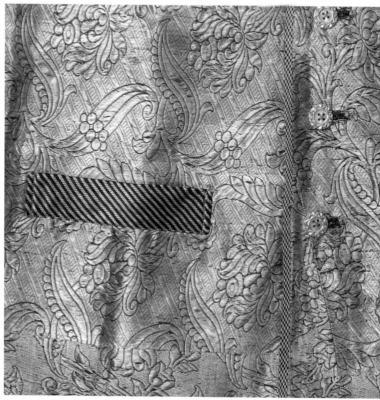

Above: *Running brocade fabric was gathered and stitched to a waist band in another form of styling.*

Page 50: *Detail of an old panelled lehnga.*

Pages 48-49: *Blue lehnga from the late 18th century stitched from specially constructed woven panels with 'jungle' motifs combining a variety of animals and birds.*

within a grid so that each section could be separately replicated on the loom according to the pattern. Some *naqshabands* who were from the Sufi tradition, were especially skilled and said to have come to Varanasi from Bukhara as late as in the 18th century. The design or pattern maker was also called *naqshanaveez* or *vinkar*. The head of a weaving establishment that employed weavers under him was known as a *grihast*. The simple weaver is a *karigar* or *bunkar*. The person who punches the cards as per the design is known as the *patthakati*.

Women called *tanharis* set the warp on the beam. They usually prepared about a kilogram of yarn daily and were paid for every kilogram they tied. The person who cut away the extraneous yarn on the reverse of the cloth is called the *katorna*. Depending on the design and technique required to execute it, a single length of fabric, be it a sari or a shawl, goes through the hands of eighteen people from start to finish, including the ironing of the finished piece, for which the *dhobi* is a recognized and respected member of the process.

The Master Naqshaband of Banaras Brocade, a book by Dr Anjan Chakraverty, a professor of Fine Arts in Varanasi, is a publication of recent vintage that documents the life's work of Ali Hasan alias Kalloo Hafiz. He describes the sophisticated sensibilities of weavers who give names such as *kapursafed*, camphor white, *makkai*, creamy corn and *subzkishmish*, young raisins, to differentiate the subtleties within a particular colour. Such elegance of language comes only when persons are deeply associated with their work for generations. They could offer ideas

Pages 52-53: *The traditional pattern artist is called a naqshaband. He plots the layout or motif on graph paper and sometimes has a small version made on a frame.*

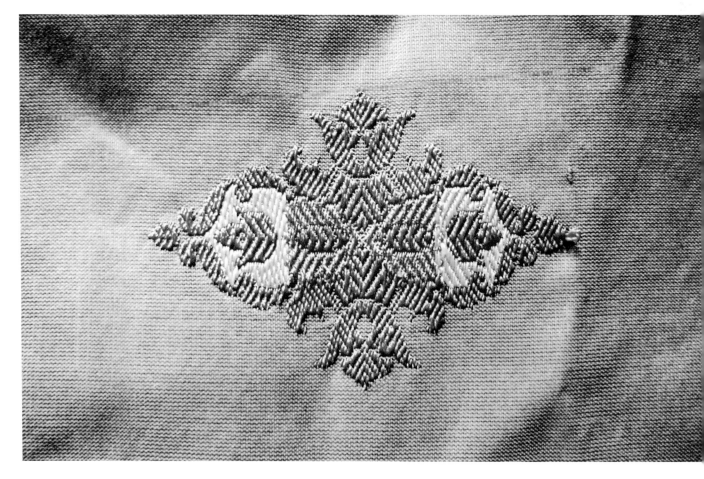

to czars of the international fashion world who impose western colour palettes for each fashion season over producers across the world to ensure their commercial interests and market domination.

The Ansaris who were weavers and the Chhipas or Khatris who were block printers, all belonging to the world of textile making, learned to live with and depend upon members of the Hindu trading community. Many Muslim weavers controlled the wholesale and retail trade in textiles along with their Hindu counterparts.

Royal courts commissioned ornate fabrics for stitched garments like robes, jackets and skirts. Hindu women preferred unstitched draped clothing, which meant saris and veils, while both Hindu and Muslim men ordered textiles for sashes, turbans and cummerbunds. Some even draped some shawls on their shoulders.

Even in the 16th century, Varanasi was still considered a thriving hub of the hand woven textile industry, not just in the city but in larger areas spreading to Gorakhpur, Maunathbhanjan, Chandauli, Mirzapur and Azamgarh districts.

It is believed that the strong induction of silk yarn into the process of weaving came about in the 17th century when silk weavers from Gujarat migrated to Varanasi after the famine of 1603.

However, the skill of brocade weaving had already developed during the Mughal period. Many of these brocades form part of the courtly dresses and furnishings depicted in the miniature paintings of Rajasthan, which also developed and flourished in the Mughal period.

Since Islam did not encourage the depiction of figures of humans, the motifs during the Mughal period changed drastically to favour flower and trellis motifs and geometrical designs. Animals were rarely depicted and humans never.

Occasionally a stylized hunting scene called *shikargah* is reproduced on carpets or hangings, and single animals like the lion

and deer can be seen. Birds were also a part of occasional ornamentation. The 'Mughal *buti*' as it is still known, came on to carpets, fabrics for garments, saris, sashes, veils and even turban cloths. Courtly nobles ordered hundreds of yards of *zari* fabric from Varanasi as turban material. The paisley also came in its Persian form, shaped like an adornment for the turban, but translated in the Indian context into the *kairi*, *amli* or *ambi* describing the shape of a mango, or the *badam,* as it was termed in Kashmir, where almond orchards flourished.

Pages 54-55: *The paisley can be arranged in myriad ways by a naqshaband. Two graphs show different versions, one with floral designs and another with script in Devanagari calligraphy to reveal a Kabir bhajan.*

Pages 56-57: *Detail of a lehnga panel woven in the early 19th century and combines the kunia, peacock, parrot, tiger, deer, trellis, fruit, flower and emblem-like patterns probably commissioned by courtly patrons.*

Pages 58-59: *A range of Varanasi brocade motifs based on Mughal tastes, developed by naqshabands, the pattern-maker, for saris, dupattas, cummerbunds and other textiles, and in popular use since then.*

Stitched garments became popular because of the Mughal custom of having tailors cut and stitch jackets and pyjamas. Hindu women did not take easily to stitched garments made popular by the Mughal courts, since the cloth needed to be measured against the human body which meant the likelihood of being touched by male tailors.

Varanasi brocades with or without gold or silver threads were therefore produced in abundance for this growing clientele, keeping hundreds of weavers occupied and the *naqshabands* in great demand for new and more attractive designs. Travellers and writers from Europe like Ralph Fitch described Varanasi as a thriving centre of cotton textiles in his 16th century writings. He also noted that there was a great demand for cloth to be used as turbans. These are shown in paintings as being of silk with gold threads. Another traveller remarks upon silk canopies hung over the deity in temples. Of particular beauty were the richly defined flower, trellis and geometric motifs in silk yarn, laid amidst a heavy ground woven of

metal threads in gold and silver that gave the entire fabric an encrusted look. Many Mughal *patkas* or sashes, canopies and furnishings were woven in this technique. A collection of these textiles in prestigious museums around the world stand testimony to the high skill and pride involved in creating such elaborate pieces.

During research done for Varanasi brocades to be recognized as worthy of special protection from global imitation under the Geographical Indicators System, the writings of John-Baptiste Tavernier were found to throw light on the flourishing trade of brocades in Varanasi in the 17th century. Tavernier was a wealthy traveller and diamond merchant who found, bought and sold a 118-carat diamond that after many adventures, ended up in England as the Hope Diamond. He is said to have visited the

Page 61: *Looms of narrow width were made specially to suit the demand for turban cloth like these in cotton with zari. Red is popular with royals and bridegrooms.*

Below: *An old painting of carefully patterned and stitched courtly dress in Mughal times and adopted by Hindu noblemen.*

court of the Emperor Shah Jahan and rubbed shoulders with kings and nobles all over the world. His works described in accounts of six voyages mark him as having the eye of a cultural anthropologist. This is evident in his writings about Varanasi, which he visited in 1632. He describes Varanasi as being at the height of its prosperity and writes of having seen a serai caravan of weavers selling their fabulous textiles to customers without the intervention of middlemen. He noticed that the fabrics were graded according to quality and carried imperial seals and featured both cotton and silk. Merchants not carrying seals of approval were flogged for avoiding checks for high quality production. Fabrics included saris, *dupattas*, cummerbunds, and turbans. Tavernier remarks upon the Bindumadhava temple in Varanasi where silken brocaded cloth, most likely to have been woven locally, hung over the holy platform. Along with temple decorations and hangings, these silken wonders formed a part of palace furnishings and wardrobes of the elite as exports from Varanasi reached all parts of the world.

Page 63: *The words in Urdu script of Kabir the weaver poet of the 15th century is woven in jamdani style at the ends of a stole made for a special project in 2012.*

Below: *In the 20th century, modern trends such as stripes combined with traditional borders for saris began to appear.*

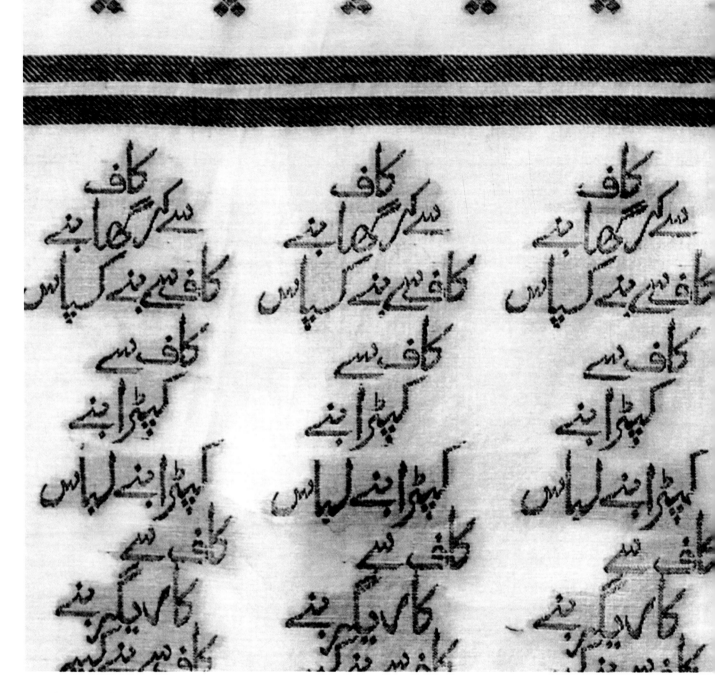

Kabir: The Weaver Poet

The history of fabric in Varanasi at this time is incomplete without recounting the remarkable personality and contribution of Sant Kabir, who lived from 1440 to 1518.

He was a weaver, a poet-philosopher, a mystic and a cult figure who remains in the hearts of all weavers and believers in social harmony and a spiritually superior way of life. Kabir was said to have been born of a Brahmin widow. If this had been public knowledge it would have had extremely detrimental social consequences for his mother. It is quite likely that this may have been the reason because of which she abandoned him.

He was found by a poor Muslim weaver couple named Neeru and Nima who named

him Kabir or Kabira, meaning the great one, from the Arabic name 'al-Kabir' after the 37th God in Islam. There are many legends about events in his life. Some like to say he was born of virgin birth, (undoubtedly the legend was created to cover the stigma of being illegitimate), and found by a muslim couple, floating on a lotus leaf.

It is also said that the only word he could write was 'Rama' as he remained illiterate, but in reality it can be said that he was brought up with love and care by his foster parents and seemed to have developed faculties far beyond their capacity to teach.

His religious teachings were under a Hindu teacher called Guru Ramananda. This helped him in his development as a person reaching out beyond religion and taking the best from the major religions of the time. Legend also has it that when he died, there was a fight between his Hindu and Muslim followers about the mode of the last rites.

The Muslims wanted him buried, while the Hindus wanted to cremate him. When they finally removed the shroud from his body they found a pile of flowers lying underneath it instead of his body. The dispute was settled when one group buried some of the flowers and the other burned them. The manifestation of this legend is visible today in Varanasi in the form of a tomb for the Muslims and a *samadhi* (memorial) for the Hindus which are placed side by side.

Kabir preached through songs in the form of poems or couplets about all human beings being equal, thereby rejecting the caste system. He sang of how they should live their lives to reach ultimate salvation, which combined karma and the idea of merging oneself with the ultimate God.

He combined both Hindu and Muslim premises, while also borrowing from Sufi traditions and bringing Sikh followers into his fold. He stirred everyone with the simplicity and power of his ideas and the use of simple, rustic phrases connected with his own profession of weaving.

The most well-known of his poems, popularized by classical and contemporary musicians in India and recited by American poet Robert Bly, is about weaving, dyeing and wearing the cloth in a way that one does not sully it. It is a metaphor for leading a pure life and becoming one with God at the end.

Page 64: *Zari threads create Kabir's poem in Devanagari script on a cream base of fine silken fabric.*

(1) kabīrā jab ham paidā hue
jaga haṅse ham roye
aisī karanī kara calo
ham haṅse jaga roye

chadariyā jhinī re jhinī
he rāma nāma rasa bhinī

(2) aṣṭa kamalā ka carkhā banāyā
pañca tattva kī pūnī
nava dasa māsa bunana ko lāge
mūrakha mailī kinhī

(3) jaba morī chādara bana ghara āyā
raṅga reja ko dinhī
aisā raṅga raṅgā raṅgare ne
lālo lāla kar dinhī

(4) cādara oḍha śaṅka mat kariyo
yeh do dina tumko dinhī
mūrakha loga bheda nahi jāne
din din mailī kinhī

(5) dhruva prahlāda sudāmā ne oḍhi
śukadeva ne nirmala kinhī
dāsa kabīra ne aisī oḍhī
jyoṅ kī tyoṅ dhara dinhī

Above: *Variations of the Kabir stoles demonstrate the fine lines of a script in cutwork.*
Below: *Weaver at work.*

Translation

1) When I was born, the world smiled and I cried. However, I will do such deeds that when I leave, I will be the one smiling and the world will be crying. This life is like a very thin transparent shawl which should be drenched in the holy name of Lord Rama, the Reservoir of Pleasure.

2) The eight lotuses is the spinning wheel using the five earthly elements to make the *chadar* (the body). In nine of ten days, the *chadar* is completed; however, those who are fools will destroy it.

3) When the chadar is completed, it is sent to the dyer (the spiritual master) to colour it. The dyer (the spiritual master) coloured it as such that it is all red (the colour of self-realization).

4) Do not have doubts or fears while wearing this *chadar*. It is only given to you for two days and it is temporary too. The foolish people do not understand the temporariness of this *chadar*, and they day by day destroy it.

5) Great devotees such as Dhruva Maharaja, Prahlad Maharaja, Sudama, and Sukadeva Goswami have worn this chadar and purified it through their lives. The servant, KabirDasa, is attempting to wear this chadar as given to him originally by his 'guru'.

For all his spiritual qualities, Kabir lived the life of an ordinary mortal. He married and had a family, unlike most ascetics, and worked among the people spreading the word of social harmony that later became a powerful force in the Bhakti movement. *Kabir: The Weaver Poet* presents novelist Jaya Madhavan's rendition of Kabir as a weaver:

> Kabir's weaves, like his poems, were expressions of his innermost feelings and thoughts. Cotton from his loom shone like silk and was smooth like satin. Kabir could spin the cotton in such a fine count that the fabric could pass through a ring.
>
> The designs he created were unusual and laid in exquisite colours. A blue stretch of cloth would look like a sliver of the Ganga itself, so much so people called it abrawan, 'running water'—for if you carelessly let the material adrift in the river, it would be impossible to distinguish the floating fabric from the running water. If he wove in brown, it would capture the very texture of the earth.
>
> 'Does Kabir weave cloth or magic?' some wondered. 'Maybe Kabir knows sorcery and lures the five elements to breathe life into his fabrics,' commented the malicious ones. Yet everybody looked forward to Kabir's weaves at the Friday market, if not to buy them then just to gape at the splendid creations. But today Kabir had spent more time than usual at the ghat and was late. He was headed for the market empty-handed. There would be many sad faces and sighs of disappointment.

Kabir, the weavers and Varanasi are intermingled so deeply that it is difficult to think of one without the other. Contemporary playwrights and classical singers draw from the repertoire of Kabir's songs and poems. Modern artists often use his imagery. While an enlightened society are respectful of his legacy, there is an aura of neglect around his memory in the daily life of the city of Varanasi.

However, today, Kabir Math, an institution dedicated to the life and teachings of this simple and humble weaver who is revered as a saint stands at Kabir Chaura and Lahartala near Lal Ghat in Varanasi.

A cult called the Kabir Panth has followers who live by his teachings and spread his word.

Muslim weavers can recite his bhajans in Hindi as easily as his dohas in Urdu but in their work they are compelled to follow what the market dictates.

Left: *A stamp issued in 1952 to honour Kabir was worth 9 paise, now a denomination no longer in use.*

Page 68: *A screen was painted in 2012 depicting Kabir as the great weaver and unifier in society, whose golden words emerge from his loom.*

Above: *Even when blouses were stitched, the style adopted by Hindu women allowed for a free size that could be tied in front to suit the wearer. Varanasi textiles with lightly brocaded patterns were popularly used for this style in the early 20th century.*

Page 71: *Royal matriarchs of Kerala, who habitually wore only creamy white, zari lined handloom decked themselves up in Varanasi brocades for ceremonial occasions during British times.*

British History

The flowering of Varanasi's silk and cotton textiles under the Mughals was in complete contrast to the fate of Indian weavers ever since the East India Company was established and brought about the colonization of India by the British. This happened not just in Varanasi but also in other parts of the country as well. The Industrial Revolution in Britain became the catalyst for British goods, particularly textiles manufactured by machine in Manchester and Lancashire, to be imported freely into India, while throttling Indian exports of crafts and textiles through high taxes. British manufacturers wanted to push their textiles in the markets of Africa and Asia. India was not just a huge market, but a supplier of cotton yarn for them as well. Protectionism in Britain led to the total impoverishment of Indian weavers and the great brocades of Varanasi continued only because of domestic courtly patronage and the continuing demand for saris from the women of India, especially as bridal wear. Interestingly, while handlooms were being decimated, documentation of textile traditions went up as British rulers established gazetteers and made a practice of noting local conditions in every sphere of activity. British travellers also came in large numbers to see the new jewel in their realm and examine its various wonders. They also remarked about the fabulous Indian textiles in their writings.

The study by the Human Welfare Association that works among weavers in Varanasi, has listed many such notings of those times. George Annesley, 2nd Earl of Mountnorris (1770 – 1844), called Viscount Valentia, was a British peer and politician who travelled eastwards to India, Ceylon and the Red Sea. Valentia is supposed to have indulged in textile trade as well, and conducted a *durbar* in Varanasi where those who attended brought some exceptional examples of *zari* and brocades. He surmised that they were only meant to be worn by prosperous people on important occasions and that the prosperity of the people of Varanasi rested on the exports of these textiles to Europe. He also wrote of them as 'expensive and showed close patterns'.

Another document that refers to the weavers of Varanasi is the report of a Mr Deane, a civil servant posted as Collector of Varanasi in the early 19th century in which he lists the number of handloom and carpet weavers who produced silks and brocades at that time.

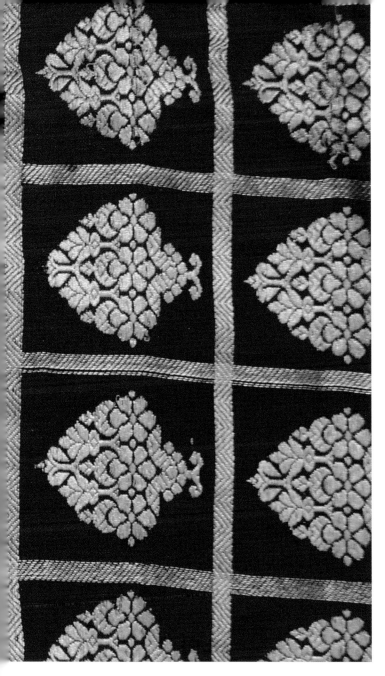

Government Gazetteers of the regions of Agra and Oudh brought out in 1922, give a count of more than thirteen thousand weavers getting employment from handlooms in the city of Varanasi. Tales are told of a certain weaver named Subhaanmiya from Varanasi whose specially commissioned fabric was sent to Queen Victoria for her birthday celebrations.

A Britisher named CGM Birdwood, a sensitive lover of the arts and student of the social systems of India, published a book called *The Arts of India* in 1880. After referring with admiration to the existing skills of Indian crafts people, he expresses his dismay at the rapid industrialization of India through textile mills in Bombay as well competition from the textiles of Manchester. He writes:

> But of late, these handicraftsmen, for the sake of whose works the whole world has been ceaselessly pouring its bullion for 3,000 years into India, and who, for all the marvelous tissues and embroidery they have wrought, have polluted no rivers, deformed no pleasing prospects, nor poisoned any air; whose skill and individuality the training of countless generations has developed to the highest perfection; these hereditary handicraftsmen are being everywhere gathered from their democratic village communities in hundreds and thousands into the colossal mills of Bombay, to drudge in gangs for tempting wages, at manufacturing piece goods, in competition with Manchester, in the production of which they are no more intellectually and morally concerned than the grinder of a barrel organ in the tunes turned out from them.

Cotton weaving in Varanasi was the starting point and highlight of its handloom tradition for many centuries. However in listing the industrial arts of India in his book, Birdwood points to the study done by Dr Forbes Watson titled *The Textiles Manufacturers and the Costumes of the Peoples of India*. He describes it as 'embodying the research and work of a lifetime', and finds references to the cottons of Oudh, the Deccan and also including Lucknow. However, Watson nowhere mentions Varanasi. It may indicate that fine cotton production had come to an end or that Watson did not look far enough. He may have missed the semi-

Pages 72-73: *Textile for a sari or canopy in red silk and brocade woven during the late 19th century is no longer woven because of its fine patterning and complicated layout.*

skilled weavers in Varanasi and adjoining areas who continued to produce simple loin cloths and *gamchhas*. The latter is a scarf used by toiling labourers in multiple ways such as a turban, scarf, waistband or towel as required by the moment at hand. The production of these continued unscathed till the late 20th century since it was not affected by imports or export policies put into place later. However by the early 21st century the ubiquitous *gamchha* began to be displaced by cheaper mechanised imports dumped in piles on village and city streets to attract passing customers.

It is clear that these Britishers were lamenting the loss of the courtly brocades and had bypassed the cotton weaver who exists and struggles even in contemporary times. He faces mechanized competition from not just industrial cities but machines located across developing nations which provide cheap labour in less than congenial factory conditions. Under the section title 'Silks', Birdwood finally brings up the word 'kincob' *(kinkhab)*. Here his theories are fascinating as he describes, 'The traditional descent of the kincobs of Benaras through the looms of Babylon, Tyre and Alexandria from designs and technical methods which probably, in prehistoric times, originated in India itself, and were known by the Hindus already in the times of the Code of Manu, and before the date of the Ramayana and Mahabharata'.

After demonstrating through descriptions of textiles that seemed to be replicas of those brocades and 'kincobs' made in India in Homer's famous poem *The Iliad*, Birdwood finally laments the policies of the British government in the following heartfelt words:

Pages 74-75: *A patka, a sash or scarf, worn by men of nobility. It is variously recognized as kinkhab or minakari in which the motif is embedded in a field of zari to replicate enameling.*

When the old East India Company began to import Indian silks with other Eastern stuffs to England, a great deal of exasperation was felt by the home manufacturers of cotton, wool and silken goods; and at length the Legislature of this country was constrained to pass a scandalous law of 1700 already mentioned, by which it was enacted 'that from and after the 29th day of September, 1701, all wrought silks, Bengals, and stuffs mixed with silk or herbs, of the manufacture of China, Persia, or the East Indies, and all calicoes, painted, dyed, printed or stained there, which are or shall be imported into this kingdom, shall not be worn or otherwise used in Great Britain; and all goods imported after that day, shall be warehoused or exported again'.

Will Durant, the famous Pulitzer Prize winning author of *The Story of Civilization* travelled through India in the course of his study to write this monumental work during British rule. He came across the impoverishment of Indian skills and industry which made him angry. It stirred him enough to take time off from his larger study to write a small book called *A Case for India,* which is little known since the British banned it. It remerged only in the 20th century when a patriotic Indian bookseller called TN Shanbagh reprinted it at his own cost in Mumbai. This short but powerful work documents British policies of exclusion and social scorn, its cruel taxation of the people of India to fund its wars elsewhere and the crushing of the Hindu spirit to benefit British industry and through denial of education to those whom they had impoverished. He writes, 'Instead of encouraging education, the Government encouraged alcohol, as the

Pages 76-77: An all-over brocade and zari sari, combining stylized flower and paisley motifs. The pattern was created during the British period. It is one of the designs that is now no longer woven because of its elaborate character.

East India Company made handsome profits from the trade.' Durant does not just express sentiment but buttresses every statement with facts and figures of how India was emaciated and crushed. The handloom weavers of India were among the larger groups to be affected by such policies since they directly affected British economic interests.

Handlooms lay in the doldrums for most of the British period, except for some special pieces commissioned for the royal court. They began to look up only after India achieved Independence. Mahatma Gandhi with many of his followers committed themselves to reviving weaving skills to provide employment and give strength to both the rural economy and poor handloom weavers all across the country.

From hundreds of thousands of looms, Varanasi's weaving population dwindled to a couple of hundred thousand, and now, in the early 21st century, stands at about thirty or forty thousand, with many looms lying idle. It can be argued however, that despite all these disasters, the Indian woman has remained loyal to the Varanasi sari that must be part of her wedding day or at least her

trousseau. Weavers too have worked hard to innovate. They now produce dress material and ready-to-be-tailored 'suit pieces for the modern Indian Woman.

There would be no fabulous Varanasi brocades today without Muslim master crafts men who have continued to work and build upon their ancestral skills and without the Indian woman's perennial love for the 'Banarasi brocade' sari.

Master weavers turned entrepreneurs like Maqbool Hassan of Resham Silks in Varanasi have not just nurtured age-old traditions but developed fine new pashmina weaves and silk-wool brocades.

Alongside, he has established a school for 1,500 girls and holds a respected position in society. Spectacular fabric actually woven out of peacock feathers is sold by Kasim Silks in Varanasi at Rs 2,000 per metre and goes to the oil-rich countries for the sheikhs to upholster their sofas. Another sari trader, SayedBhai of Taj Estate indulges his passion for exotic multi-hued birds, importing them

Page 78: *The effective contemporary layouts are those that closely follow traditional techniques and motifs. Here the weaver has placed the lotus flower at odds with the flow of the body pattern.*

at considerable sums of money so that they can strut and flap outside his four-storied sari showroom in the heart of Varanasi.

Big time designers go to master weavers and traders who produce finely woven shimmering silks, ordering special colours and weaves exclusively under their name for export, but they are enjoined to keep these secret. The film industry of Mumbai now christened Bollywood creates a great demand for shimmering Varanasi textiles and television too does not fall too far behind in dressing its male and female actors in glamorous brocades sourced in Varanasi.

Even while the antiquity and fame of Varanasi's handlooms have been established, economic and cultural developments within the past two hundred years, quite apart from colonization, have brought further challenges to the doorsteps of traditional handloom weavers. This is partly because of changing technology allowing for mechanized imitations, fast changing patterns of dress and lifestyle influenced by fashions from the West, and stiff competition from cheaper mechanized alternatives and imitation that circulate in global markets. The handloom weaver is losing his hold over customers who are aesthetically less discerning and who are not interested in matters such as engaging with traditional skills or preserving their heritage. For these clients, a much less expensive imitation 'banarasi' or dress fabric, shimmering, almost garish, is fine, even if it is made in far away China. If the Varanasi trader sells it, they will buy it.

Page 81: *The influence of chinoiserie made an appearance in a sari woven in the mid 20th century.*

Below: *Yardage created for stitched garments like men's achkans, preferred by nobility during and subsequent to the Moghul era, has the chaudani pattern all over.*

Types of Looms

Simple descriptions of different types of looms in use in Varanasi may be useful in understanding the extent of labour, skill and technique required in any form of handloom weaving. Basically, any loom is a mechanism by which vertical threads, the warp or *tana*, are stretched tight in a framework which is secured at one end so that the weft threads, *bana*, can be passed through them horizontally, integrating the two to form a sheet of fabric of desired length and width depending on the size of the framework.

The basic movement of weaving consists of different methods of passing the weft back and forth from left to right continuously till the piece is complete. A shuttle pulled by a string or thrown by hand does this. All looms that do not employ power through electricity are termed handlooms. Reproduced here are the descriptions of various types of looms formulated by textile expert Christa Kowalczyk who freely shares her knowledge through articles on the internet.

Page 82: Traditionally, women do not sit on the loom in Varanasi. However, for economic reasons women now lend a hand in any part of the process to expedite production.

Draw Looms

The first and original loom was a vertically twist-weighted type, where threads are hung from a wooden piece or branch or affixed to the floor or ground. The weft threads are manually shoved into position or pushed through a rod that also becomes the shuttle. Raising and lowering each warp thread one by one is needed in the beginning. It is done by inserting a piece of rod to create a shack.

The early Indian draw looms show a similarity to the Iranian one of the present day. It has harness structures for the base ground and another for the pattern to be imposed on this ground. Cross cords hanging from above lift the warp threads according to the pattern as laid out by the *naqshaband*. The framed harness is called a *jala* for its net-like appearance as yarns criss cross downwards from the upper frame.

Above: *Women of all ages are part of the process of handloom weaving.*
Page 85, left: *Adjusting the cards that manipulate the design on a jacquard loom.*
Page 85, right: *An elderly weaver works on a pit loom.*

An assistant is required to lift the selected draw cords attached to the cross cords, giving the loom the alternate name of a 'dobby.' This comes from the shortening of the word 'draw boy', the person who assists the main weaver.

Pit Looms

A pit loom is positioned about a foot off the floor over a pit about three feet deep in which the weaver places his legs to work the treadles.

Horizontal ground looms permit the warp threads to be chained between a couple of rows of dowels. The weaver needs to bend forward to perform the task easily.

Backstrap Looms

They are well recognized for their portability. The one end of this loom type is secured around the waist of the weaver and the other end is attached around a fixed thing like door, stake, or tree. Pressure applied to the yarn can be customized by simply bending backwards.

Frame Looms

Frame looms have almost the same mechanism as ground looms. The loom is made of rods and panels fastened at right angles to construct a form similar to a box to make it more handy and manageable. This type of loom is used even until now because of its economy and portability. Many weavers who now get opportunities to travel abroad to demonstrate their weaving techniques fabricate miniature frame looms for convenience. This enables them to show the customer the extent of skill required to weave their fabric and enhances its economic value. The reality of handweaving comes alive in constrast to factory production. Some frame looms are now made of metal.

Jacquard Looms

Apart from these traditional looms, Joseph Marie Jacquard used some existing innovations and mechanisms to create the jacquard loom and weaving technique in the middle of the 18th century. The traditional draw loom was complicated, as it required two persons to operate. The warp ends had to be picked up manually by one person as the other operated the shuttle. Multiple rows of holes are punched on each card, each row of which corresponds to one row of the design and the many cards that compose the design of the textile are strung together. An average sari uses 1500 to 2500 cards while a more elaborate pattern would raise the number of cards ten-fold. Jacquard designs on saris tend to have a slightly mechanized look.

The jacquard is a mechanism rather than a loom. It is more a 'head' that could be attached to a power loom or a handloom. The head controlled which warp thread is to be raised during shedding. Multiple shuttles could be used to control the colour of the weft during picking. Since the new jacquard method allowed for the yarn to be picked up according to the required pattern, it was possible to create a greater number of complicated designs.

Many weaving establishments converted to the jacquard loom from the draw loom. The carding system replaced the fine drawings of the *naqshaband*, although they still formulated

Below: *Detail of a punched card used on a jacquard loom. It predates the arrival of a computer card.*

the basic layout, which got transferred to a system much like the computer. Only one person is needed to operate the flying shuttle. Further technological progress brought about by the Bonas Machine Company, which launched the first electronic jacquard in 1983, has far overtaken the capabilities of the individual weaver and increases the capacity of the machine significantly. According to experts, it enables single end warp control to extend to more than 10,000 warp ends and avoids the need for repeats and symmetrical designs and allows almost infinite versatility. The computer-controlled machine significantly reduces the down time associated with changing punched paper designs as well.

Above and below: *Weaver at work*

In a world of rapidly changing technology, electronics and digitization, and even computer-designed patterns, the weaver is left struggling with incomprehension as his known skills become redundant, and many processes in production cut short.

Rising costs of yarn and production justify cost cutting methods but the grand tradition of handloom weaving, with its exquisite fabrics that amazed the world from the middle of the 15th century till the late 19th century, are now treasured skills that demonstrate an intangible heritage that must be preserved, if nothing but to demonstrate the sheer skill of the human hand and an aesthetic imagination that comes from the heart.

Pages 88-89: *Bobbins indicate the weaver is preparing a sari in the kadua technique.*

Powerlooms

The real source of trouble for the handloom world was mechanization in the form of the powerloom. It came into being after a series of innovators worked to create a machine that could run on power.

This allowed the many textile mills employing cotton handloom weavers of Manchester and Lancashire to raise production and demand larger markets.

It normally takes from seven days to three months to weave a handloom sari, whereas seven or eight saris can be produced from the powerloom in one day. This was the major reason for the decimation of the vast and famous handloom tradition of Varanasi.

A ballad about the poor displaced handloom weavers in those areas of England in the 17th century expresses the emotions of their Indian counterparts:

Handloom Versus Powerloom

Come all you cotton weavers, your looms you may pull down. You must get employment in factories, in country or in town.

For our cotton masters have a wonderful new scheme: These calico goods now wove by hand, they're going to weave by steam.

In comes the gruff o'er looker, or the masters will attend. It's 'You must find another shop or quickly you must mend.

Such work as this will never do, so now I'll tell you plain: We must have good pincop-spinning or we ne'er can weave by steam.'

There's sow-makers and dressers and some are making warps. These poor pincop-spinners they must mind their flats and sharps.

For if an end slips under, as sometimes perchance it may, they'll daub you down in black and white and you've a shilling to pay.

In comes the surly winder. Her cops they are all marred. They are all snarls and soft bad ends, for I've roved off many a yard.

I'm sure I'll tell the master or the joss when he comes in. They'll daub you down and you must pay, so money comes rolling in.

The weavers' turn will next come on, for they must not escape. To enlarge the master's fortune, they are fined in every shape.

For thin places or bad edges, a go or else a float, They'll daub you down and you must pay three pence or else a groat.

If you go into a loom shop where there's three or four pairs of looms, They all are standing empty, a-cluttering up the rooms.

And if you ask the reason why, t'ould mother will tell you plain: 'My daughters have forsaken them and gone to weave by steam.'

So come all you cotton weavers, you must rise up very soon, For you must work in factories from morning until noon.

You mustn't walk in your garden for two or three hours a day, For you must stand at their command and keep your shuttles in play.

From Folk Songs and Ballads Of Lancashire, (Oak Publications, 1973)

Pages 90-91: *A powerloom works much faster and multiplies production while putting handloom weavers in difficulty.*

In the 20th century, the Sulzer loom from Switzerland created panic among weaver's organizations in India since the production from one large loom could displace the daily output of forty-five handloom weavers. China's determined push to enhance its economic power globally has led to hundreds of Sulzer looms being set up in China in the mid 21st century, copying, among other styles and techniques of India, the famed Varanasi brocades.

Age-old designs are brought out through computerized methods in a fraction of a second and at a tenth of the cost of the hand-made original which had been finely honed through generations of skill and creativity. The result can be seen on the downcast faces of hundreds of weavers across Varanasi and its environs.

Handlooms fight back valiantly even in the 21st century, but most owners of weaving establishments now invest in powerlooms and keep them along with handlooms often under one roof. Pit looms are visible, but tend to get flooded if the lanes nearby overflow during the monsoons.

Most weavers work on jacquard looms. Power outages are a regular feature even in modern Varanasi, so when the powerlooms come to a stand still: when the room is dark even though the handloom weavers cannot see well, lanterns and gas lamps can be rigged up to keep the handlooms working in semi darkness.

Electricity is a boon, even if the powerloom has replaced handlooms, one advantage being that a tiny television can be perched against the frame for the weaver to watch a cricket match or a Bollywood film to take him away to a dreamland from the drudgery of his manual work. It is only the senior, highly skilled master weavers who not only speak nostalgically about intricate weaves, but also make the effort to find younger workers who are willing to apply themselves to learning complicated techniques and weaving high quality fabric. All types of looms as described can be seen at weaver's establishments within the city of Varanasi and adjoining villages.

Page 92: *Weavers closely examine their designs every time they take a pause from weaving at the Weavers Service Centre in Varanasi.*

The important fact to remember is that most looms are not owned by the weaver sitting at them but by the owner of the establishment or workshop. This *grihasti* or master weaver, may have been born into a weaver's family and mastered the art, but eventually had the resources and spirit of enterprise to move upwards into business and trading. When such a person employs others to work for him, he is more sympathetic of their needs and problems than people who simply move in to trade in any form of textile.

Such a person also understands how to translate the demands of designers for his weaver to execute. Often, urban designers are unaware of the intricacies of different weaving techniques and create patterns on paper or computers that are impossible to translate in to a textile. Sometimes the master weaver is looked upon as a 'middle man' but he is not always exploitative as is made out.

Pages 94-95: *Handlooms in Varanasi, as elsewhere in the country, occupy spaces crowded with stacks of cards or other looms.*

Weaving Techniques

Silk yarn has always been imported from different parts of India and even abroad and carries the name *parai*, meaning 'from the outside' or 'outside'. Bangalore and Kashmir have been mulberry growers and silk producers for long, and were among the earlier suppliers of yarn. Finer qualities were imported from Japan and China. Today most of the yarn comes from China, and is held by local cartels that control prices to the detriment of weavers. Government bodies set up yarn banks but access and distribution according to fair methods still remain a problem.

The yarn is boiled to remove the gum left by the silk worm, till it attains a floss-like quality. It is sorted and tied into hanks. These are dyed in a variety of brilliant colours. The yarn is then wound onto a wooden five-spoke wheel before being wound onto spindles. Tradition has it that the new bride of the family would settle the unruly yarn, while the oldest woman in the family would wind the thread around the first bobbin.

Page 96: *Bobbins with silken thread await the weaver's use.*

It is interesting that women are customarily involved at the beginning of the process and are the ultimate wearers of the sari as well. Other textile researchers like Jasleen Dhamija have come across traditions that require the shroud, *kafan*, in which a weaver is wrapped when being prepared for burial to be woven by the brother-in-law of the deceased. He also weaves the *dhakana*, or veil, to be worn by the weaver's widow.

Cultural patterns connected with birth, celebrations and death, philosophical teachings, songs and as importantly, professional earnings, are all inextricably bound in Varanasi around the process of weaving cloth.

Varanasi is well known for its different styles of weaving created to obtain patterns termed as brocade. The basic technique is to create a supplementary weft that overlays the woven

Above: *Spools of silk thread lie at the weavers fingers waiting for a pattern to be executed.*

Page 98: *A model wearing a contemporary creation sits among more traditional citizens from Varanasi.*

cloth with its warp and weft as the base. The extra weft is passed through the warp by means of heddles to lift the pre-arranged extra warp threads to make a raised pattern of motifs, which may be floral or geometric, paisley or trellised.

The area without a pattern is skipped, revealing the base weave underneath. The pattern emerges in low relief and can be done in silk or with gold and silver thread. It presents a textured effect rather like embroidery. Sometimes gold and silver threads are part of the basic warp and weft or part of the overlay.

When the patterns are in plain silk threads, they give an embedded appearance. When the silk background is hardly visible because it is overlaid solidly with gold and silver, the fabric is called a *kinkhab*. If the background is entirely gold or silver and the pattern is in silk, it is called *minakari*.

The most elaborate embroidered look in a brocade is described as *kadwa*. In a brocaded piece the reverse will show sections of loose threads joining one patterned area to another. These are left as they are or cut away by specially trained cutters who do not damage the base cloth.

Jamdani is a technique shared by weavers in Uttar Pradesh and West Bengal and Dhaka in Bangladesh. Varanasi excels in this form of brocading which has silk as the base cloth but cotton in the brocaded pattern. It may or may not have some additional ornamentation in gold and silver threads.

Page 100: *Silk brocade cutwork.*
Below: *A jamdani weave.*

The cotton weft threads are fixed between a number of warp threads to achieve a pattern.

A typical sari will have floral, trellis, or *jali* (lattice) designs with a prominent border above and below and an extravagant end piece called the *pallu*, which may also add a *konia*, or corner piece of a paisley or floral motif at two corners where the *pallu* begins.

Some of the familiar and evocative names for jamdani designs include *chameli*, jasmine, *pannahazaar*, thousand emeralds, *gendabuti*, the marigold motif, *pan buti*, heart or betel leaf shaped motif, and *tircha*, which refers to the pattern when it is placed diagonally.

The *Jangla* could be described as an extravagant type of brocade in which the pattern spreads boldly across the entire fabric. They are usually in bright hues.

Muga or golden coloured raw silk is used instead of *zari* threads. Commonly descriptive names are *bel* (trellis), *buti* (flower motif), and *jali* (lattice).

Tissue is the technique of making the entire cloth translucent and golden. This is done by laying silk and gold threads across the entire body, in both warp and weft.

Gold or silken threads form the brocaded patterns laid over this base. Tissue is most popularly used as veils over wedding saris, and when used with a thicker count of silk becomes a stunning wedding sari, shot with silk threads in either red, orange or pink.

Pages 102-103: *A jangla pattern in brocade weaving that covers the ground of the entire fabric.*

Jamawar tanchoi is also termed *tanchoi*. These are silk on silk brocades with an extra weft silk for the patterning. Saris are in pastel colours, often with a monochrome effect. Finer, smaller patterns usually cover the entire surface.

As in the jamdani, a smaller amount of silk or gold *zari* is added as an enhancing embellishment. The *jamawar* shawl tradition of Kashmir inspires designs having elongated or entwined paisleys or trellis patterns— hence the name *jamawar tanchoi*. According to researcher Dr Chakraverty, the name *tanchoi* has an interesting history.

Above: *Kora, cotton with zari in cutwork.*
Page 105: *A pale tanchoi weave is the technique of brocading without zari, normally in closely merging colours.*

Apparently the three Chinese brothers of the Choi family came to Varanasi to sell silk. It is likely that one of them was named Tran Choi. Weavers claim that the name of this textile is a corruption of the Chinese name.

Cutwork is locally called *katrua* and is actually a simplified form of jamdani in which the pattern is not incidentally spread out but runs from edge to edge. Any part of the thread on the reverse side that does not form part of the intended pattern remains untidily attached to the main cloth, with the loose ends left floating till the piece is taken off the loom. Cutters then get to work elaborately and carefully cutting away the extra threads.

Buti daris derived from *buti* which is a flower but has come to mean a design with scattered flowers, leaves, birds, paisley motifs, circles or chevrons developed from Mughal times. Most *butis* have their own names, which are listed for common use in combination with straight or diagonal stripes, in clusters or scattered singly across the entire fabric. Some of the formal names are *mehrab, ashrafi, angoor, resha, kairi, gulab, kamal* and with the suffix of *buti* or *bel* attached depending on whether it was a single motif or a trellis.

Pages 106-107: *Contemporary jamdani techniques moved to geometric patterns. Small and large butis are typical of brocade weaving on saris and stoles.*

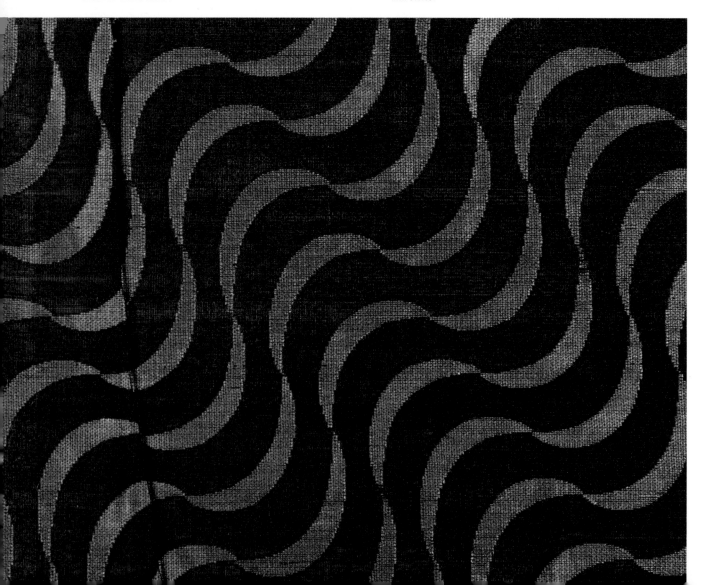

Zari Making

Zari is the gold or silver thread used for weaving or embroidery. In earlier times when precious metals were not so costly, real silver was used and given a gold wash or plating. Old *zari* saris were melted down into real silver after the silk threads in between began to wear away. The original method was to melt down a pure silver ingot to make wire or strips called *pasa,* which were beaten to form wire not more than 13 microns in width. Four hundred kilometers of *zari* wire contained 1 kilogram of silver. The process was so elaborate that it took sixty persons, twenty-two days to complete this length of *zari*. The strip was flattened and used as such. This was called *badla.*

The easier and more common technique was to roll or wind the flattened metal wire around silk threads or cotton threads. It was then electroplated with gold. This is called *kallabattu* or *kasab.* Today *zari* is made both in Varanasi and Surat in Gujarat.

High costs have made *zari* makers use polyester threads. Artificial or 'tested' *zari* is made out of softer, malleable copper wire instead of silver, and burnished with colour to give the effect of silver or gold. Most of the market is flooded with this artificial *zari,* which gives sparkle at low cost, but is devoid of the sophistication obtained from the sober sheen of real *zari.*

Page 108, left: *The River Ganga shimmers in the early morning sunlight as if woven with zari threads.*

Page 108 (right), and Page 109 (all images): *The process of zari making is tedious but provides the material that enriches most of the textiles that emerge from Varanasi.*

Handlooms, Continuity and the River Ganga

Varanasi takes pride in the fact that it is the single oldest city enjoying the stability of a continued and active existence from the time of its inception. Other cities have risen and fallen but something about Varanasi defies such courses of history. While the traditions of textile weaving is ancient as well, the stability of its foundations has been shaken considerably. From a bird's eye view, it is clear that the heavy boots of technology and competition have taken a big toll. Add to these the crushing blow of colonization at the hands of a Britain that was in the first flush of the industrial revolution, aggressively asserting its political and economic domination over its colonies across the world.

The sheer energy and force of combustion engines and machines powered by gas, steam and electricity in Britain and other Western countries swept away the noble and meticulous efforts of generations of weavers existing through the strength of their handwork. Mahatma Gandhi's dictum of machines removing drudgery but not being allowed to displace man's dignified and honourable work hardly worked against this onslaught. The British heard his call for a non-violent struggle for freedom but ignored the philosophy behind his call for compassionate, egalitarian, honourable employment systems across society. Free India has not fully heeded the import of his words either. It struggles to keep people out of poverty but its policies become a part of the great one-size-fits-all process of globalization.

Page 110: The powerful, silent flow of the great River Ganga dominates the consciousness of Varanasi at all times of the day.

In this new world, it is not just old-fashioned mechanization but computers, digital automation and electronic data production that have taken over modes of production.

These have flown completely over the heads of all but half a dozen weavers in Varanasi. Even these fortunate ones who have had occasion to travel the world and see what modernity is all about, only lament how China has computerized and imitated them out of their profession.

They nostalgically remember their visits to the Victoria and Albert Museum or the Textile Museum in Washington DC where they spotted the splendid weaves of their forefathers displayed in all their glory.

Above: *A zari border edging on a contemporary sari needs no other embellishment. Its drape flows like the river itself.*

Page 113: *Discussions on the marketibility of newly designed stoles take place within the trading establishment.*

They click pictures of such brocades on their mobile phones, enlarge them on return to India at the nearest digital photo shop in Varanasi, frame them behind shiny plastic sheeting, and hang them on their showroom walls, amongst old certificates and awards, to point out to visitors with whom they do business.

Tiny villages around Varanasi like Sarai Mohana, a short walk across a side stream of the Ganga, finds weavers caught between despair, drink and a wild hope that a miracle worker will come to provide raw material, orders and markets. Their sons have gone away to Dubai in search of survival or work in the city at a mobile phone repair shops.

Cholapur, a few miles beyond the outskirts of the other side of the town has well supervised work on more than a dozen looms, with innovative designs given by textile designers who are trying to marry tradition to contemporary tastes, and even enticing modern urban women to take pride again in wearing a 'Banarasi' sari.

Master weavers, *grihastas* and *gaddidars*, the Hindu and Muslim traders (named as such because they sit on *gaddis*, mattresses), are the lifeline of the weaver at the loom. They feel a strong sense of responsibility towards their weavers. They know that if they do not provide continuous work, or advance them money for a family wedding or funeral, they may lose them forever. Even if there is no work, they will develop new designs for the new season and reach out to textile designers in Mumbai, Delhi and Kolkata, to develop some exclusive

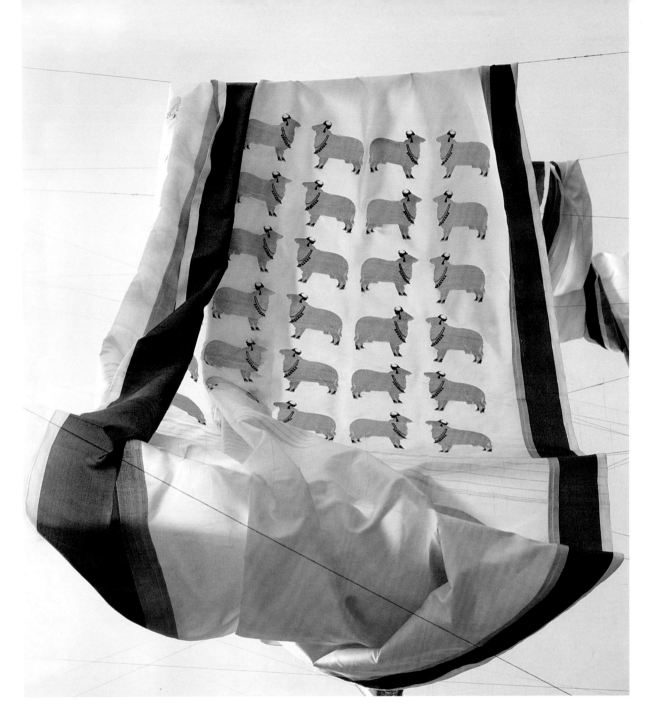

designs for faraway markets. In the early part of the 21st century, unsubstantiated but perturbing news spread through the media and the developed world that some weavers of Varanasi had committed suicide because of poverty and loss of markets. A well-known international fashion house called Bestseller stepped in to finance a project to infuse funds and hope into the homes and hearts of the weaving establishments. A major order for 14,000 stoles was executed, and projects set up in adjoining villages to develop fine export quality cotton fabric. It helped some survive but most others are still struggling. Master weavers recognize the value of their tradition and are committed to keeping it alive.

Pages 114-115: *Handlooms from the famed city of Varanasi will survive as long as they are re-invented, re-vitalized and keep ahead of cheaper imitations. Contemporary innovations have enticed many fashion conscious women who tend to look to the west for acceptability to return to the sari as the most attractive fashion statement.*

Pages 116-117: *A replica of an old lehnga using the tiger motifs of an earlier era.*

Pages 118-119: *Stoles are new accessories that enjoy wide appeal in India and abroad. They have enabled Varanasi weavers to regain hope in their work. Designs are a mix of the traditional brocades and dramatic geometric layouts that embellish any outfit.*

Small lanes dotted with shops selling Varanasi saris bought from small weavers across the city attract thousands of visitors who come to Varanasi to pray at the Kashi Vishwanath temple or attend a *bhajan* (group singing of devotional songs). Festivals of classical music and dance add to the magic of the ghats and remind people of the strong cultural traditions of the city.

European, British and American backpackers, Japanese or Korean Buddhists, students of religion and others who have simply been attracted by the idea of Varanasi's sacredness and antiquity often forget that antiquity itself is composed of many threads, influences, cultures, people and thought. The handloom tradition is one such important thread that should be woven into the entire fabric of this city.

Below: *Yarn spun from feathers shed by peacocks in nearby forests are woven into fabric that delight customers from the Middle East. The multi-hued sheen is both subtle and lustrous.*

Kabir's humanitarian and all-encompassing philosophy of life is waiting to be rediscovered, just as the skills and potential of the weavers of Varanasi need reinventing.

The mighty Ganga has become polluted with all the indiscriminate waste that goes its way. Global imitations and marketing create a form of pollution of the textile tradition. These forces cannot be allowed to wipe away the history of Varanasi, still living, working, creating and amazing those who explore and discover the shining fabrics that emerge out of its nooks and crannies. An example of this can be illustrated through the peacock motif which is a reccurring feature in many textiles of Varanasi. Feathers shed by this magnificent bird are gathered from fields and forests nearby and turned into yarn. This is woven into a luminous multi-hued cloth that is both organic and wondrous. It represents the spirit and ingenuity of the Varanasi weaver who refuses to be forgotten.

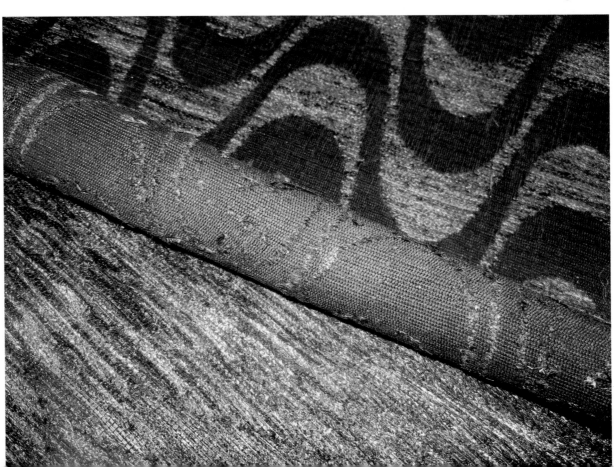

Above: *The eternally popular peacock motif on a contemporary silk sari is derived from a Picchwai painting. While the origin of the motif is traditional Rajasthani art from Nathdwara, the Varanasi weavers make it their own.*

Handlooms, Continuity and the River Ganga   121

Acknowledgements

Varanasi is a very welcoming city. Whenever you visit a weaver's establishment, you will be shown all kinds of new and old fabrics, told many stories, and offered many cups of tea. It will be difficult to resist buying a beautiful silken stole or brocaded sari.

Among the many helpful friends in the handloom community, I must thank Badruddin Ansari of Kasim Silks, Sayed Bhai of Taj Estates, Maqbool Hassan of Resham Silks, Haji Anwar Ahmed of Danish Collection, Iqbal Kausar of Bodey Textiles, Parwaaz Silk Sarees, Javed Akhtar of H Farooque Selection, Mohd Ibrahim of Haji Munna Banaras Handicraft, HA Nasir Ansari of Silk Heritage, Mukund Bhai of Prabha Traders, Hasin Mohd of HM Textiles and Girija Shankar Niraj of Nilambari for providing swatches showing different weaving techniques. Silk textiles are also printed in a few establishments. The friends at Rangoli Prints in the heart of Peeli Kothi in Varanasi's weaving area showed us a wide range of experiments in silk and wool, hand block printed for further embellishment.

The Weaver's Service Centre with Mohammmad Yasin as its co-ordinator, was helpful in demonstrating its revival and development work. He took us to Cholapur, a small village among wheat fields on the outskirts of the city, where work goes on at a good pace. Anjali Pathak, a keen organic farming expert and nature lover of Lucknow made sure I visited Serai Mohana village across the Ganga opposite the beautiful J Krishnamurti Foundation estate where peacocks dance and a sense of peace and quiet prevails. At Serai Mohana weavers are divided between those who work for the Taj Group of Hotels and those whose sons have lost hope and gone to Dubai in search of earnings, or struggle to make ends meet by working in a mobile phone or cycle repair shop in the city. I thank them for attending a meeting and sharing their problems with me. I gave them the advance I received for this book to buy yarn to produce some newly designed stoles for sale, but it neither brought an outcome nor lifted their spirits.

Arupa Majumdar, the Librarian, and Rajendra Singh, the curator, at the Bharat Kala Bhavan at Banaras Hindu University were extremely courteous. They assisted in accessing two old articles, *Sadiyon me saadi Banarsi saadi* by Anuradha Singh and *Banarsi sari udyog: Savaal Asmita ki,* by Rajendra Kumar Dube, which helped trace the antiquity of the weaving tradition in Varanasi.

Dr Rajnikant of Human Welfare Association shared his passionate concern for the welfare of weavers and requested me to conduct a public hearing for them a few years ago. Listening to their many tales of woe could have been a wholly tragic occasion except for their dark humour and indomitable will to survive that kept breaking through the gloom. Their insights proved invaluable. Dr Rajnikant was one of the applicants for the GI registration of Banarasi silks.

Shiv Kumar, a political activist of the democratic socialist movement arranged many meetings and trips to weavers during my work on this book. He accompanied me to their workplaces and homes and faithfully follows up on any work I request him to do with them.

Uma Prajapati of Upasana Design Studio and I, through the Dastkari Haat Samiti, joined hands to undertake the Bestseller project to help weavers in distress. Meera Mehta, a senior textile designer, worked closely with us towards creating 14,000 stoles for its employees for Christmas. Maqbool Bhai at Resham Silks and his big team of workers completed this superhuman task in a short time. Uma has provided many images taken during this project and has very graciously granted permission for use of stills from their video on Varanasi Weaves.

All weaver's establishments mentioned earlier generously gave swatches of their best work.

Sanjay Garg of Raw Mango is a highly talented designer who strongly believes in carrying on the sari tradition. His looms in Varanasi are among the most contemporary and vivacious. I thank him for generously sharing his photographs, his workspace, his collection of old textiles and his new designs for this publication.

Nishy Singh, a caring textile designer who sometimes works in Varanasi to induce pessimistic weavers to take on new challenges also provided pictures for this publication. I thank her for doing so.

My gratitude also goes to Purnima Rai, Sonal Mansingh and Rekha Shankar for lending me their treasured textiles to photograph. A special thanks to Charu Verma for sharing family textiles and using her skills at photography.

Prannoy Sarkar photographed scraps of old and contemporary textiles so that they looked their best in the aesthetic environs of the Raw Mango studio.

Tultul and Bikash Niyogi of Niyogi Books have been very patient during the process of bringing out this publication. I thank them for their enthusiasm and support which never falters.

Bibliography

Birdwood, C.G.M., The Arts of India, Rupa & Co, 1988

Chakraverty, Anjan, *The Master Naqshaband of Banaras Brocades*, monograph sponsored by the Office of the Development Commissioner of Handicrafts, Ministry of Textiles, Government of India, 2002

Chattopadhyay Kamaladevi, *Handicrafts of India*, Published by Indian Council for Cultural Relations, 1975

Crill Rosemary, Ed., *Textiles from India*, Seagull Books, 2006

Dhamija, Jasleen, and Jain, Jyotindra, Ed, *Handwoven Fabrics of India*, Mapin Publishing Pvt Ltd,1989

Irwin, John & Jayakar, Pupul, *Textiles and Ornaments of India*, a MOMA Publication, Ayers Company Publishers Inc, 1972

Jaitly, Jaya, *Varanasi weavers lost in an urban and global jungle*, in *The Other Side*, a monthly journal of socialist thought and action, May 2008

Jayakar, Pupul, *Textiles and Embroideries of India*, Marg Publications,1956

Jaitly, Romanie, *Tanabana, Handwoven and Handcrafted Textiles of India*, Ministry of Textiles, Government of India, 2007

The Master Weavers, a catalogue for the Festival of India in Britain, 1982

Madhavan Jaya, *Kabir, the Weaver Poet*, Tulika Publishers, 2010

Report Submitted by the Human Welfare Association to the Textile Committee for certification of Geographical Indicators, 2007

Tavernier, Jean Baptiste, *Travels in India*, Delhi Reprint, 1995

Uttar Pradesh Gazetteer, 1922 & 1965

Photo Credits

Bitan De Niyogi: *18, 20, 21, 22, 26, 27, 41*

Charu Verma: *11, 12, 51, 70, 81, 118*

Dastkari Haat Samiti: *63, 64, 66-67 above, 68*

Jaya Jaitly: *13, 40, 42 top right and below, 43, 44, 46, 52 centre, 53 above right and below, 55, 71, 84, 92, 100, 101, 108 left, 113, 120*

Nishy Singh: *85 right, 87 top, 108 right*

Prannoy Sarkar: *8, 14-15, 24-25, 31, 32-33, 34, 35, 36-37, 38-39, 47, 48-49, 50, 56-57, 58, 61, 62, 72-73, 74-75, 76-77, 78, 80, 102-103, 105, 112-115, 116-117, 119, 121*

Sanjay Garg: *98, cover*

Trisha De Niyogi: *28, 29, 110*

Upasana Design Studio: *10, 42 above left, 45, 52 top and below, 53 above left, 54, 59, 60, 66-67 below, 82, 87, 85 left, 86, 87 below, 88, 89, 90-91, 94, 95, 96, 99, 100, 104, 106, 107, 109*

http://indianraga.wordpress.com: *69*

Glossary

Rumal - Coverlet, Kerchief, usually square

Mothra - Jasmine buds

Chaudani pallu - Diamond-shaped twill design on the end piece

Naqshaband - Pattern makers

Gaddidars - Hindu and Muslim traders (named as such because they sit on *gaddis*, mattresses)

Kumkum - Vermilion powder

Nilambari - Textile in a particular shade of blue-black depicting the night sky

Butis - Flower motif

Zari - Mettalic thread

Ghat - Series of steps leading down to a body of water

Moksha - Salvation

Ganga Maiyya - Mother Ganga, the River Ganga or Ganges

Jal - Water

Hiranya - Gold cloth

Tantuvay/Tantividyas - Weaver

Siri - Female weaver

Kinkhab/Kincob - Brocade with a gold or silver base into which a pattern is embeded

Neevi - Undergarments

Baharivas - Cloth which was worn to cover the body rather like what is known today as the *chadar* or shawl

Chadar - Shawl

Adivas - Shawl in the Rig Vedas

Angutranika, kasikavastra, kasikansu, kasikurtam,

Kashya - Cotton textiles

Kasek, Varankasek - Silk cloth

Hiranya Vastra, Putambar Vastra - Fabric woven in Varanasi as referred to in Hindu literature

Kasikuttama, Kasiya - Textiles of Varanasi in Buddhist literature

Divyavadan - A Buddhist text

Kasikamsu - Textile of Varanasi

Varaseyaka - Fine textured fabric of Varanasi

Kasika Suchivastra - A kind of embroidery which could have been an embellished or raised form of weaving in Varanasi

Kasayanivastrani - Simple robes of a monk

Thiugyamo - Resplendent brocade

Gyaser - Brocade textile used in Buddhist establishments

Tankha - A painted scroll of spiritual imporatnce usually framed with *gyaser*

Naqshanaveez/Vinkar - Designer or pattern maker

Grihast - The head of a weaving establishment

Karigar - Worker/Artisan

Bunkar - Weaver

Patthakati - Person who punches the card as per the design

Tanharis - Women who set the warp on the beam

Katorna - Person who cuts away the extraneous yarn on the reverse of the cloth

Dhobi - Washerman

Kapursafed - Camphor white

Makkai - Creamy corn

Subzkishmish - Young raisins

Shikargah - Stylized hunting scene

Kairi, Ambi, Badam - Mango or Almond shape

Patkas - Sashes

Samadhi - Memorial

Durbar - Court of a ruler

Gamchha - All-purpose scarf

Tana - Warp

Bana - Weft

Jala - Net

Parai - Outside, foreign

Kafan - Shroud

Dhakana - Veil, cover

Minakari - Silk pattern embedded into a gold or silver ground

Kadwa - Elaborate embroidered look in a brocade

Jali - Lattice

Pallu - End piece, usually of a sari

Konia - Corner design before the end piece begins

Pannahazar - Thousand emeralds

Gendabuti - Marigold motif

Pan buti - Heart or betel leaf shaped motif

Tircha - Diagonal

Jangla - Ground pattern, usually extravagantly spread across the entire fabric

Muga - Golden coloured raw silk

Bel - Trellis

Tanchoi - Silk on silk pattern

Jamawar Tanchoi - A tanchoi pattern inspired by the jamawar shawl tradition of Kashmir

Katrua - Cutwork

Buti daris - *Buti daris* derived from *buti*

Mehrab - Archway

Ashrafi - Coin

Angoor - Bunch of Grapes

Resha - Silken threads

Kairi - Mango

Gulab - Rose

Kamal - Lotus

Pasa - A technique to melt silver in the zari making process

Badla - Metal or Zari strip

Kallabattu/Kasab - The technique of rolling or winding the flattened metal in the zari making process

Grihastas - Master weavers

Gaddi - Mattress

Bhajan - Devotional song

Lehnga - Flared skirt

Dupatta - Long Scarf

Index